Dallas

Dallas

Mixed Verse from a Shooting

Jeff Hood

RESOURCE *Publications* · Eugene, Oregon

DALLAS
Mixed Verse from a Shooting

Copyright © 2017 Jeff Hood. All rights reserved. Except for brief quotations in critical publications or reviews, no part of this book may be reproduced in any manner without prior written permission from the publisher. Write: Permissions, Wipf and Stock Publishers, 199 W. 8th Ave., Suite 3, Eugene, OR 97401.

Resource Publications
An Imprint of Wipf and Stock Publishers
199 W. 8th Ave., Suite 3
Eugene, OR 97401

www.wipfandstock.com

PAPERBACK ISBN: 978-1-5326-1664-8
HARDCOVER ISBN: 978-1-4982-4052-9
EBOOK ISBN: 978-1-4982-4051-2

Manufactured in the U.S.A.   JANUARY 12, 2017

For the Victims of Dallas

Babel.

After
The Huffington Post
July 18, 2016

WRITING USED TO BE easy. Now, nothing seems easy. Leaning in, I just stare at the screen. Occasionally, I try to type something. Despite my desperation to write, my mind is held captive to a former place.
Bloody films never leave you. Every image sticks. The officer took his gun and shot Alton Sterling dead. Amidst the screams, Philando Castile bled out. Everyone wanted to talk about their lives, I couldn't get past their deaths. I wasn't alone. We put out a call. Over a thousand people responded. Downtown Dallas has been the site of dozens and dozens of rallies. Over the last year, we've repeatedly marched for endangered lives. The rally was large. We didn't hesitate. The crowd was ready to go. The speakers were ready to go. We were ready to go. Cries of justice rang out.

In the midst of misery, God is incarnate. When we believe all is lost, God speaks from the bones. The bones rise up and lead us on. They did that night.

I was nervous about speaking. When I opened my mouth, everything seemed clear. Though I spoke for a long time, people have only remembered one phrase, "God Damn White America." The gathered understood the adaptation of Jeremiah Wright's infamous phrasing. The message of unity was simple. The message of love was heard. We must become one. There is no White America. There is only America. Violence has a way of creating confusion.

Fear is not a part of faith. I didn't care. I was afraid.

Safety was at the front of my mind. The Dallas Police Department guided the marchers through downtown with tremendous grace. On multiple occasions, we stopped or changed routes to make sure that everyone had the chance to keep up. I stayed at the front of the line. In time, I settled into the rhythm of the movement. Throughout the march, anything seemed possible. Love and justice was within our grasp. Then, confusion reigned.

Darkness was all Jesus knew. The disciples professed their allegiance to him. Now, they couldn't even stay awake. Unable to function, Jesus cried out in fear. No one was woke.

Our march wound through downtown. Stopping at the Old Courthouse, we took a minute to talk about the 1910 lynching of Allen Brooks. There was no denying that the march for love and justice was long. For a few seconds, I stared at the bricks. What did they know? What would they say? How much further is the journey? Organizers and the police shouted for me to run up to the front of the march. I did.

For the next few blocks, I talked to a DPD Sergeant. In the midst of the rally and protest winding down, we talked about the success of the night. The conversation felt natural. There seemed to be a genuine connection. A few steps past Austin St., everything changed.

Things seemed clearer before Babel. Now, no one speaks the same language. Confusion is all anyone knows.

"Pop-pop-pop-pop-pop . . ." I heard it so clearly. I've heard it ever since. The shots rang out. The violence was all that was clear. Bullets flew in every direction. Multiple people dropped. The echoes only enhanced the terror of it all. Pandemonium took over. Grabbing my shirt to make sure I hadn't been shot, I ran back toward the protestors. I was terrified that a thousand people were about to walk into the middle of a shootout. Throughout the evening, I carried a 10-foot cross. At this moment, I used it as a shepherd's staff and started swinging it around. Screaming, "Run! Run! Run! Active Shooter! Active Shooter! Active Shooter!" I got as many people out of there as I could.

The march was beautiful. Every step was about stopping violence. Love and justice seemed so loud and so close. Evil didn't listen. 5 Officers were Dead. Devastation set in.

Total confusion arrived.

For the next few days, I told my story on every major news outlet in the country and beyond. The officers were never far from my mind. Repeatedly, I reminded people that this was a nonviolent peaceful protest. "Love" and "justice" were the only words on my lips. I looked directly into the camera and declared, "Stop shooting America!" I don't know if anyone heard me. Violence always confuses the ears. I saw it happen. I saw it happen again in Baton Rouge. Former words are confused and present words are confusing. We will not be able to understand until we stand down.

Oh God, deliver us from Babel.

Amen.

Relearning to Think

After
Baptist News Global
August 4, 2016

The world was in chaos.

I stood before a huge crowd. There were only seconds to go before it was time for me to speak. I stepped up to the bullhorn. I spoke as passionately as I ever have. Victims of police brutality filled our minds.

Feet constantly hit the pavement. Hundreds and hundreds of souls yearning for justice marched down the glowing streets of Dallas. Energy was high. I could feel it in my bones. Whispers of hope filled the air. The diners stood in reverence. Nobody was able to avert their eyes. Endurance mingled with the heat. Sweat dropped to the pavement. There was no stopping us. We wanted justice. God was there somewhere.

Old bricks pulled us forward. Centuries of injustice drew us together. The historic Dallas County Courthouse is a mound of red rock cascading to the sky. The back steps were a fitting place to remember — a place where on a day in the past, the screams for blood had grown louder and louder. After fighting their way into the courthouse, several thousand people dragged Allen Brooks out of his trial. Not long after, the mob lynched Brooks. Throughout the day, his body was on display. Postcards were created to commemorate the event. Though it happened in 1910, my brain felt like it was closer than I could have ever dreamed. The hanging. The dragging. The hating.

"Jeff!" I snapped out of it. I had to lead everyone back to where we started. Running up front, I took my position with the large cross that I'd carried most of the night. After a few moments, we started walking.

The chants had subsided. Everyone just seemed to be humming. Divine buzz surrounded us. The major and I chatted about how positive the night had been. Everything seemed to be fine. Though I was still in strong spirits, I was very tired. Any event of this size or magnitude really takes the wind out of the organizers. My brain seemed to be slowing down in anticipation of the end of the protest. Then, shots. Time stopped.

Ringing. Ringing. Ringing. I'd never heard a noise so consistent. In the distance, I saw multiple people drop to the ground. Shots. It took me another second to figure out what was going on. When I realized that someone was shooting, I stared into the distance. Shots. I picked up my cross and swung around. Echoes surrounded me. I didn't know where the shots were coming from. I didn't know who was going to be next. I just knew that there were hundreds of people behind me that were potential victims. Lowering my cross to a staff, I ran to get as many people out of there as I could. Parts of my brain are still on Commerce Street.

Cameras were everywhere. Everyone wanted to talk. From early in the morning until late at night, I did interviews in the scorching heat. Flashbacks of the night before kept running through my brain. Shots. Terror. Desperation. The images cycled around and around. It wasn't like watching a movie. It hasn't been since. The images are more like a kaleidoscope. The colors are slightly distorted and repeatedly cycling. My brain just won't snap out of it. Throughout the day, I recalled everything I knew. Even when I didn't want to remember, I forced my brain to work. It was important that the world knew that we held a nonviolent protest that was sabotaged. Though I had no problem telling the details of what I experienced, I still couldn't figure out how it happened. I just wanted to talk about love and justice. How did these officers get killed? Though the world demanded more and more details, I needed to grab hold of my brain. I was tired. I was devastated. I was on. "Rev. Hood, what happened last night?"

Time sped up. The threats were endless. Life seemed to blur. Death lurked behind every door. The phone continued to ring incessantly with interview requests. My brain wasn't working. Thoughts wouldn't form. Talking seemed difficult. I started to receive police protection. Our five children under the age of 4 were not fooled. Consistently, our children demanded answers. I demanded answers of myself. I couldn't figure out how these officers were dead. There was no amount of exercises or counseling that could get my brain thinking correctly. It didn't matter. I had a sermon to preach. "We are called to give our bodies to the struggle against injustice."

Weeks passed. Trauma grew. I still hear the gunshots. I still feel the terror. I still see the faces of the fallen. Slowly, I am relearning to think. It's almost like I have to catch my thoughts and wrestle them to the ground. Even though it's difficult, I haven't stopped thinking. I know the world needs thinkers right now. Just last Sunday, I was reminded why I still work to think.

Before I could get out the door, my young son said, "Please, Daddy, don't get shot in Dallas."

The shots.

The world is still in chaos.

Amen.

I'll never forget that night. I was unprepared. I guess anybody would've been. I'm still unprepared to write at greater length than the blogs I've already shared. Maybe I can do that later. Regardless, this is a collection of verse that came to me as the events transpired. Dallas, Texas is a violent place. Every bit of it was revealed on the 7th of July.

Mixed Prayers
My Office
July 5, 2016

Fear struck

There was nothing to fear
I could've stayed right there
I'd been working so hard
I could've stayed right there
Somebody had to lead
But I could've stayed right there
I didn't

My brain wouldn't stop
An innocent man was dead
I started making the calls
To plan a response
Where was the peace
Out in the street
I had to do something
I moved

Again

My Office
July 5, 2016

Shots rang out

I saw it all
The man on the ground
Dead over some bullshit
When will it stop

Hands up, don't shoot
No justice, no peace
I'd heard all the slogans

Alton Sterling bled out
Because we forgot to shout
We could've stopped this
We could've pushed back
Didn't we realize we were under attack

Now we're just left with a bloody tape

I couldn't be silent

Alton Sterling
My Office
July 5, 2016

Right on cue
It didn't take long
All of a sudden
The press jumped on

The problem was that they had the wrong guy
No innocent man deserves to die
But there it was
I watched it played out
How could there be any doubt
Alton Sterling didn't deserve to die

Police

My Office
July 5, 2016

Fuck the police
It's not that easy
I know a couple good cops
Who would never drop
Anyone over some bullshit stop

Organizing
My Office
July 6, 2016

We talked all night
Who would be with us
Who had the passion
Who had stamina
To get us to the end
Who had the intellegince
To steer the movement
After some talk back
We reached a conclusion
We needed the same voices
That'd always been our choices

Philando Castile

My Office
July 6, 2016

That white t-shirt
The blood flowing down
Everybody called you
They knew you were cool
What do these cops take us for
Some damn fools

But this time the crime's on tape
I'm praying that justice won't be late
I'm drowning in all this hate
The event is growing
Our voices won't be slowing

Numbers

My Office
July 7, 2016

Two videos
Made the numbers grow
Philando in the car
Alton on the ground
Both gunned down
Police on the radio
The bullets shattered
Black skin
Racism exposed
Everybody knows
The truth
Dallas is as bad
As either of these towns
The numbers grew
The rally was going to be huge

Better Prepared

Belo Gardens Park
July 7, 2016

You promised to help
I waited on you
There were things I had to do
Where's the sound system
I couldn't hear anything
Where's the security
I couldn't see anything
I can't believe I trusted you on all this shit
We're starting out buried in a pit
Why can't you be better prepared
Ok, there's no need to fight
We're here for justice tonight

Interviews

Belo Gardens Park
July 7, 2016

I wasn't the only one
Excited about the night
The local media swarmed
To try and get the facts right
Do you expect a big crowd
Yes
Are people angry
Yes

Young Man on the Bench

Belo Gardens Park
July 7, 2016

You spoke up
I'd never seen you before
You asked how I got here
You knew my name
You told me everything
You told me that things would never be the same
How did you know
It's like you knew every step before I took it
God was near
I heard something in my head
I am with you always

Christian

Between
July 7, 2016

You are my friend
We did it all
Traveled nationwide
Stood against the fall
We talked that afternoon
We thought we knew what was coming
We didn't have a clue

Parked

Between
July 7, 2016

We moved the car
Not very far
We just needed the place
To be in a safe space
We didn't move the car far enough

Closer

Belo Gardens Park
July 7, 2016

Is there room
Will anyone come
Did we exaggerate
People will come
One person
Ten people
Forty people
The trickle turns to a flood
Hundreds and hundreds
Are we ready
They are

Familiar Speakers

The Rally
July 7, 2016

One pushes back
One reaches out
One gets mixed up
One carries the dream
One gets the facts out
One screams
One
That's what we were that night
One
One people speaking one truth
Justice

The Hill

The Rally
July 7, 2016

You're not real
I once thought you might be
But there's nothing real about you
Yet, there we were
Standing on something artificial
Trying to deliver a real message

The Pastor in the Crowd

The Rally
July 7, 2016

Speaking loud
I looked down
I saw the pastor
Cowards of cowards
Surprised to see him
I shrugged
I tried not to care
I did
Where in the hell had he been?
Go back to the hole you slithered out of.

Angry Words

The Rally
July 7, 2016

We played our part
Spoke the anger
In our heart

Black Lives Matter

The Rally
July 7, 2016

All lives matter
We knew that was a lie
Black lives matter
We screamed it out into the sky
That's what everybody said
Didn't all the others know
Two blacks folks were dead
Black lives matter
Nothing else

God Damn White America

The Rally
July 7, 2016

I was about to speak
I thought I knew what to say
Then a different voice came into my head
It sounded divine
Now was the time
Channel Jeremiah Wright
I did
God Damn White America
The most controversial words I've ever spoken
They were true

Prayerful Utterances

The Rally
July 7, 2016

These weren't normal prayers
Fuck this or that
Don't usually count
Damnations
Are considered anathema
Everyone wants orchestrated prayers
Nobody just says what needs to be said
We did
We held our future in prayer

Electioneering

The Rally
July 7, 2016

Who is this
Does she think this is a game
This ain't no damn election
Real lives are at stake

Guns

The Rally
July 7, 2016

Why did you bring those damn guns?
This is a peaceful protest.
Put that shit up.
Are you trying to get us killed?

The Sgt.
The March
July 7, 2016

We were in charge.
We talked the whole time.

You saw us.
You didn't judge us.
You were with us.
You were really with us.

I'll never forget your words.

The March

The March
July 7, 2016

Hand in hand
Arm in arm
Voices united
We were all there
We were all there together
We marched

Every street was ours
Every intersection was ours
Every corner was ours
Every step changed the world
We didn't stop
We marched

One body
One mind
One heart
One moment
We marched

What happened to us
Where did we go
How did it happen
We never stopped
We marched

The streets were our scripture
The movement our God
The steps our revelation
The promise our salvation
The Spirit was with us
We marched

The Faces in the Restaurants

The March
July 7, 2016

We marched past you.
Were you with us?
We couldn't tell.
Some of you clapped.
Some of you waved.
Some of you stood at attention.
Some of you cheered.
Some of you did all sorts of things.
You were the faces in the restaurants.
But, were you with us?
I guess you went back to eating your steaks.
I imagine that caviar tasted mighty fine.
One more glass of wine!
We marched past you.
Where were you at the end?

Louder and Louder

The March
July 7, 2016

The steps grew louder.
The cries grew louder.
The claps grew louder.
We grew louder and louder.
If noise could change the world.
Maybe it did.

The Eye

The March
July 7, 2016

Eye ran back
Eye was worried
Eye couldn't find Emily
Eye just wanted to see her
Eye was overwhelmed
Eye saw her in the distance
Eye embraced her
Eye was sure she was ok
Eye ran back
Eye had a march to lead
Eye had no idea what was coming
Eye just kept on marching

Steps

The March
July 7, 2016

We knew we weren't safe
We just kept marching
Love was in the air
We just kept marching
Anger was everywhere
We just kept marching
Police marched close
We just kept marching
Strangers surrounded us
We just kept marching
The way seemed long
We just kept marching
Feet were growing tired
We just kept marching
Mouths shouted out
We just kept marching
People were offended
We just kept marching
The news was grim
We just kept marching
The pain was real
We just kept marching
Confusion crept in
We just kept marching
Louder and louder
We just kept marching
There was great power
We just kept marching
In spite of it all
We just kept marching

Where are we going?

The March
July 7, 2016

Where are we going?
I thought you knew the way?
Where are we going?
Will things always be this way?
Where are we going?
Is this the right way?
Where are we going?
Do we have to keep going this way?
There were no answers.
We simply kept marching.
The way.
This way.

The Shooter
The March
July 7, 2016

You were standing there.
I never saw you.
You knew what was next.
I never saw you.
We walked right past you.
I never saw you.
We gathered for justice.
I never saw you.
They heard us.
I never saw you.
They were ready to listen.
I never saw you.
I organized the event.
I never saw you.
I guided the march.
I never saw you.
Am I blind?
I never saw you.
Surely you could have been stopped?
I never saw you.
Should I have looked harder?
I never saw you.
We had no idea what was coming.
I never saw you.

Lynched

The Courthouse
July 7, 2016

1910
Allen Brooks
Lynched
2012
Trayvon Martin
Lynched
2012
Jordan Davis
Lynched
2013
Renisha McBride
Lynched
2014
Eric Garner
Lynched
2014
John Crawford
Lynched
2014
Michael Brown
Lynched
2014
Laquan McDonald
Lynched
2014
Tamir Rice
Lynched
2015
Freddie Gray
Lynched

2016
Alton Sterling
Lynched
2016
Philando Castile
Lynched

The Shots

The Shooting
July 7, 2016

We were talking about how well the march went.
Those were the last words that were said.
Then, the world changed.
Pow.
Pow.
Pow.
Pow.
Pow.
The shots kept flying.
You ran toward the shots.
I knew what I had to do.
I had hundreds of protestors behind me.
I had to get them out.
Pow.
Pow.
Pow.
Pow.
Pow.
The shots kept flying.
The shots changed everything.
Life would never be the same.

Shooting

The Shooting
July 7, 2016

Who's shooting?
Are you hit?
Who's shooting?
Am I hit?
Who's shooting?
Are we hit?
Who's shooting?
Are they hit?
Who's shooting?

Screams

The Shooting
July 7, 2016

I'll never forget the sounds.
I still hear them.
Chaos exploded.
Confusion exploded.
Pandemonium exploded.
All hell broke loose.
The world was one big scream.

Active Shooter

The Shooting
July 7, 2016

I turned around.
There were hundreds to save.
I started swinging the cross.

Active Shooter!!!
Active Shooter!!!
Active Shooter!!!

Run!!!
Run!!!
Run!!!

Active Shooter!!!
Active Shooter!!!
Active Shooter!!!

I ran down the street.
Hundreds ran to safety.
I just kept swinging the cross.

Active Shooter!!!
Active Shooter!!!
Active Shooter!!!

Run!!!
Run!!!
Run!!!

Active Shooter!!!
Active Shooter!!!
Active Shooter!!!

Prayers

The Shooting
July 7, 2016

People were praying in the streets.
People were praying in the alleys.
People were praying in the buildings.

Our screams were prayers.
Our shouts were prayers.
Our cries were prayers.

There were millions of prayers.

Television

After
July 7, 2016

People died.
Television revealed the truth.
I didn't know.
I was outside trying to help.
The names came later.

Lorne Ahrens.
Michael Krol.
Michael Smith.
Brent Thompson.
Patrick Zamarripa.

I was devastated.

The Station

After
July 7, 2016

I had to get to the station.
The narrative had to be right.
This was a peaceful protest.
The narrative had to be right.
We didn't do anything wrong.
The narrative had to be right.
I ran down the street.
The narrative had to be right.
I got to the station.
The narrative had to be right
I busted through the doors.
The narrative had to be right.

The First Interview
After
July 7, 2016

You opened the door.
You brought me up.
You got the mic.
We were behind the lights.
We were live.
The questions brought it all out.
I told you what I saw.
I realized I saw more than I could handle.
The cameras rolled.

Emily

After
July 8, 2016

I marched with you.
I couldn't find you.
The shots rang out.
I couldn't find you.
Chaos ensued.
I couldn't find you.
I was scared.
I couldn't find you.
My phone was dead.
I couldn't find you.
I looked for you.
I couldn't find you.
I went on television.
I couldn't find you.
You saw me.
I couldn't find you.
You came to the station.
I found you.

Sleep

After
July 8, 2016

I can't sleep.

Hour 1
Was it all a dream?
Hour 2
Was it all a dream?
Hour 3
Was it all a dream?

Rise and shine.
It's interview time.

Good Morning America

After
July 8, 2016

Good Morning America
Stop Shooting America
Good Morning America
Stop Shooting America
Death Reigns in Dallas
It Doesn't Have To
Stop Shooting America

Interviews

After
July 8, 2016

Just a few more interviews.
I have to keep going.
I have a story to share.
We were peaceful protestors.
We were demanding love and justice.
Next question.
Next interview.
Next question.
Next interview.
Next question.
Next interview.
Repeat the message.
Repeat the message.
Repeat the message.
Love and justice.
Love and justice.
Love and justice.
Just a few more questions.
I can't take it anymore.
I need to go home.
Just a few more interviews.

The Words

After
July 8, 2016

God Damn White America!
Do you regret saying this?
Knowing what I know now.
I'd have chosen different words.

The Crazies
After
July 8, 2016

Murder.
Kill.
Destroy.
Threats.
Mayhem.
The crazies are out.

Holed Up
After
July 9, 2016

Fear grows.
Threats increase.
Here at the house.
The family just left.
Complete protection.
Nowhere to be found.
Police patrol outside.
Where do I go?
Nowhere.
I'm here to stay.

The Sermon

After
July 10, 2016

I got up to preach.
Thank you for inviting me.
I've had a devastating few days.
Then, I let it rip.
Recalling police brutality, I cussed.
Thinking about failure, I screamed.
Speaking about the murdered officers, I mourned.
Dreaming of the future, I fought.
Listening for the possibilities, I believed.
The church must do something.
The church can do something.
Church!
Wake the fuck up!

Trauma

After
July 11, 2016

Heart racing.
Mind racing.
Stomach racing.
Everything is racing.
It all keeps coming back.
I can't make it stop.
Trauma.
Destroyer of life.

Downtown

After
October 7, 2016

Three months later.
I went back.
I climbed the hill.
I walked the march.
I heard the shots.
I touched my stomach.
I saw where I was.
I remembered.
I realized.
I never left.

Prayer

*After
November 7, 2016*

Where was God that night?
I don't know.
Where was God that night?
I don't know.
Where was God that night?
I don't know.

Now

After
December 7, 2016

People have moved on.
I'm still stuck there.
Standing in the street.
Feeling the shots.
Clinging to a cross.

Dallas.

Trinity Presbyterian Church
Denton, Texas
July 10, 2016

It's been a very busy time. Just a few days ago, I organized the rally and march that preceded the deaths of five police officers in Dallas. This morning I want to journey through the story of Dallas and end with in the familiar story of the Good Samaritan.

On Wednesday, I partnered with others to organize the protest. We were all disgusted at the video of Alton Sterling's death at the hands of the police in Baton Rouge, Louisiana. The next day another video showing the death of Philando Castile at the hands of police in Falcon Heights, Minnesota became widely available. Seeing those men bleed out . . . watching black Americans regularly bleed out in our streets . . . remembering Ferguson . . . remembering Baltimore . . . remembering city after city where black lives do not matter . . . including our own . . . Denton, Texas . . . is overwhelming. We see it over and over again. We see black communities overpoliced. When communities are overpoliced, there is no doubt that tragedies happen in greater frequency.

Someone asked me the other day to prove that there is police brutality in Dallas. I simply responded, "Why would a thousand people show up to protest police brutality rally if there wasn't brutality?" We never expected so many people. We thought there was going to be a hundred or so. When the video of Philando Castile bleeding out went viral, the numbers increased exponentially. We gathered at the rally. When I looked out into the sea of people, I wondered, "What does Jesus have to say in a time like this?" By traditional interpretations, the answer is absolutely nothing. We keep on offering salvation to people who are dying in the streets. We keep on talking about Jesus loving the world and we can't even take the time to love our neighbors.

We say that we are a people who believe that God loves the world . . . but look around. We don't do shit. People are being gunned down in our streets and we don't do shit. Look around! We keep on hearing people demand that the church do more. The church doesn't have anything to give. The church has no voice. The church has no witness. The church has no purpose.

We traded our voice for influence. We traded our witness for political power. We were most concerned about protecting churches. We wanted to make sure we maintained our denominations. In the mean time, we gave everything away. Do you care more about your church or denomination than you do these black bodies that are lying in our streets? If you do, you are not following Jesus . . . you are following evil. We have to wrestle with difficult questions in these difficult hours. What is salvation? What is love? What is truth? Where do we go from here? We gathered last Thursday night to wrestle with these questions and many others.

Anyone who declares that Thursday's protest should have been less angry . . . doesn't understand the daily violence facing black people in this country. People were mad as hell and they had every right to be. Many have criticized the language that I used at the rally. I declared, "God Damn White America!" I'm tired of hearing about White America. There is no White America. There is only America. I'm also tired of hearing about White Christianity. There is no White Christianity. There is only Christianity. A Christianity that is white is not Christianity. I wish a few more people would start damning everything that is contrary to love and justice.

Throughout our nation, you have heard the phrase, "Fuck the Police!" Why would people say such a thing? Have we considered that the situation has become so dire that people don't feel like they have any other language to use? Those who criticize the language of those who are being beaten and killed and don't stop to help are the enemies of Christ. People are being slaughtered in our streets. Why can't we love our neighbors as ourselves? We must get saved. We must stop police brutality. We must rip the racism from our hearts. We have to change.

As we began the march, we followed the directions of the police. At every turn and with every step, the protest was nonviolent. I remember the officers repeatedly commending the peaceful nature of the protest. I was thankful that the protest remained nonviolent. Why do you think protestors keep calling for nonviolence in this country? I think it's the same reason that I keep on calling for nonviolence . . . it's the only logical choice. Violence never achieves love or justice.

Towards the end of the march, we gathered at the Old Courthouse. After hearing about the horrific 1910 lynching of Allen Brooks from multiple speakers, we made our way back toward our starting point . . . Belo Gardens

Park. As I led our march to it's finish, I talked with a Sergeant from the police department. We talked about how successful the protest had been. I'd just passed Austin Street. I had on my white robe. I was carrying my black cross. I had on one of my favorite stoles. All of a sudden I looked up and heard... pop-pop-pop-pop-pop. I was close enough that I thought I might be shot. My first reaction was to grab my stomach. The Sergeant ran toward the shooting. The eight hundred people behind me were walking directly into the line of fire. I ran to get as many people out as I could. I repeatedly screamed, "Active Shooter! Active Shooter! Run! Run! Run!" My cross very quickly became a staff to push people out of the way. It was total chaos.

We didn't know who was shooting. We just knew that there were many shots. I remember the question that came after: "Why?" I repeatedly heard that one word question. When people asked Jesus questions of meaning, he consistently responded with answers of being. I did too. I kept telling people that we have to learn to be love and justice. We can't talk about justice without love and we can't talk about love without justice. When you start talking about peace and nonviolence you better make sure that you are talking about love and justice too. There is no peace or nonviolence without love and justice.

The 5 officers who lost their lives during the shooting remain heavy on my heart. It is difficult to experience something like this and not feel like you have some level of responsibility. There might be a million pieces of evidence to prove the contrary... but still you wonder what you could have done to prevent the tragedy. For 24 hours straight, I was on television. I didn't have time to mourn. I just had to spread the message of love and justice. I did television, newspaper and radio interviews all day long. It went on and on and on. I knew that if I didn't get the message of love and justice out... somebody else would be ready with a more sinister message. When we are silent, other messages fill the void. As followers of Jesus we are responsible for getting our message out... we are responsible for sharing the good news. If we don't, there will be other messages.

Last Friday night, I arrived home to hundreds of threats. People were looking for someone to blame. When you become a public figure in a time like this, you become a target for hate. People have said all sorts of shit. I even had someone tell me that the reason I act this way is because I'm a vegan. People can make some pretty wild connections. That's why we have to help them make the right connections.

Devastation doesn't come close to describing the totality of what I feel. I couldn't believe what happened. Noises scare me. Movement scares me. Crowds scare me. This morning I thought the car might blow up when I turned the ignition. We live in a crazy time . . . a dangerous time . . . a dark time. Jesus still has a word for such a time as this.

There were two people who saw suffering and walked on by. There were two people who saw great difficulties and walked on by. But in the midst of it all, there was the Samaritan. There was the person who stopped. There was the person who bandaged up the wounds. There was the person who held the hurting. There was the person who refused to walk by.

In the midst of great conflict, we keep on walking by. We say that we can't stop. We say that we can't talk. We say we don't have time. Where are the Samaritans amongst us? We need you now more than ever.

Amen.

I don't know that I'm free now. I just know that I've been changed.

www.ingramcontent.com/pod-product-compliance
Lightning Source LLC
LaVergne TN
LVHW021622080426
835510LV00019B/2708